JUNY 2012

Jubilee Lines

60 POETS FOR 60 YEARS

~

edited by

CAROL ANN DUFFY

faber and faber

First published in 2012
by Faber and Faber Ltd
Bloomsbury House
74–77 Great Russell Street
London WC1B 3DA

Typeset by Faber and Faber Ltd
Printed in England by CPI Group (UK) Ltd, Croydon CRO 4YY

A CIP record for this book
is available from the British Library

ISBN 978-0-571-27705-6

FSC
www.fsc.org
MIX
Paper from
responsible sources
FSC® C101712

2 4 6 8 10 9 7 5 3

Contents

~

Preface

~

Queen Elizabeth II was ten when her father became King George VI upon the abdication of his elder brother, the uncrowned Edward VIII; her father's early death, aged fifty-six, sixty years ago this year of 2012, resulted in her Coronation in Westminster Abbey, aged twenty-six, on 2 June 1953. The Queen has received twelve prime ministers, from Sir Winston Churchill to David Cameron, and she is the second longest serving British monarch after Queen Victoria. *Jubilee Lines* explores these sixty extraordinary years with a newly commissioned poem for each year, and in doing so brings together sixty UK and Commonwealth poets. In 'Winged Back', his poem for 1953, the Welsh poet Dannie Abse recalls the 'linseed willow-sound | of Compton and Edrich winning the Ashes', but a shadow falls in the next line of the poem where he reminds us that 'Elsewhere, Troy always burning'. Sure enough, Gillian Clarke and Douglas Dunn are alert not only to the embryonic rock'n'roll of Bill Haley (soon to be blown away like a dandelion clock by the arrival of Elvis Presley) but to the crises in Suez and Hungary, the 'tanks in Budapest'. (This sense of vigilance is common throughout the anthology in poems by, among others, Sean O'Brien and Robert Minhinnick.) Meanwhile, a newly-pregnant Fleur Adcock ('Pregnancy was a little bit rude') stands in the crowd during a Royal visit to her native New Zealand and Michael Longley (like Adcock, a future recipient of the Queen's Gold Medal for Poetry) reads Classics at Trinity College, Dublin where, in 1958, he first meets his wife-to-be of fifty years.

The poems offer a fascinating mix of the personal and the public, the political and the poetic. We read here of the revolution in Cuba, the Cold War, The Beatles, the assassination of President Kennedy; of Ruth Fainlight's doomed literary friendship with Sylvia Plath; of CND, feminism and *The Female Eunuch*. Wendy Cope writes humorously about hippies and Simon Armitage alliteratively about the Falklands War. Imtiaz Dharker, dancing in Glasgow to the Bee Gees, reminds us that Steve Biko, Groucho Marx, Robert Lowell and Elvis all died in 1977, by which time the Queen had been on the throne for a quarter of a century. Elsewhere, we find Ronald Reagan, John Lennon, Lester Piggott, Edward Heath, Marlene Dietrich, Saddam Hussein, Indira Ghandi, Valentina Tereshkova and (courtesy of Ian McMillan – who else? –) Barnsley Football Club. There are poems which recall the Miners' Strike, Greenham Common, the Great Storm of 1987, the Berlin Wall and the Millennium.

Amid this, the individual voices of the poets are always personal and particular and variously accessible or complex, free or formal – a truly democratic mix. Some of our best-known and senior poets are represented here alongside new or young poets at the start of their careers. Putting the poems together, 1953–2012, I was struck by how swiftly the sixty years seem to pass, compressed into the individual moments of the poems, fossils of what they were, and was reminded again that all poetry is concerned with time. The subjects of these poems range from birth to bereavement, their soundtracks include The Doors, Otis Redding and Pink Floyd; assembled, they are time-travel in words. 'We will not be this way again,' writes Antony Dunn in 'Eighteen', his poem for 1991. Jacob Polley, for 2005, writes 'suddenly you have your own | empty head in your hands'. And from Helen Mort, in her 'Anthropocene' for 2011, we read 'We've changed the world as much as asteroids | or earthquakes off-the-scale once did'.

I thank all the poets here for their generosity in participating in this project and for adding Poetry's voice to the Diamond Jubilee, 2012, in sixty poems which reflect on who we were, where we have been, and what we have done.

CAROL ANN DUFFY

JUBILEE LINES

1953

DANNIE ABSE

Winged Back

Strange the potency of a cheap dance tune.
– NOEL COWARD

One such winged me back to a different post-code,
to an England that like a translation
almost was, to my muscular days
that were marvellous being ordinary.
365 days, marvellous;

to an England where sweet-rationing ended,
where nature tamely resumed its capture
behind park railings. Few thorns. Fewer thistles;
to Vivat Regina and the linseed willow-sound
of Compton and Edrich winning the Ashes.

Elsewhere, Troy always burning. Newspaper stuff.
The recurring decimal of calamity.
Famine. Murder. Pollinating fires.
When they stubbed one out another one flared.
Statesmen lit their cigars from the embers.

They still do. With every enrichment
an injury. They bicker and banquet,
confer and dally, pull on cigars that glow
with blood-light. And the year 1953,
like the arson of Troy, is elsewhere. Ashes.

1954

FLEUR ADCOCK

The Royal Visit

I took my baby to see the Queen.
He was not yet born, but she wouldn't wait.
She was wearing an evening gown
of silver brocade, although it was lunchtime;
but then she was opening Parliament.

I had on a maternity smock –
it wasn't the thing to parade your bulge,
even for a respectable woman
like me, married more than a year.
Pregnancy was a little bit rude.

It took five minutes from my house,
facing the bulk of Tinakori Hill,
to Parliament and the sunshiny crowds.
I didn't wave, but the baby inside me
waggled his limbs in a loyal kick.

SS *Gothic* was chugging south
around the coastline to scoop up the Queen
from Bluff on a date long preordained.
Meanwhile biology and hormones
were organising my own rendezvous.

Two months later, when I'd turned twenty
and given birth, I'd find myself chanting
'I've got a B.A. and a B.A.B.Y.'
I could almost believe my life would glide on
with the smoothly oiled timing of a royal tour.

1955

GILLIAN CLARKE

Running Away to the Sea

It might have been heatstroke, the unfocussed flame
  of desire
for a name in a book, a face on the screen, the anony-
  mous
object of love. Two schoolgirls running like wildfire,
bunking off through dunes to the sea, breathless.

We were lost and free, East of Eden.
It was James Dean, Elvis, Bill Haley and the Comets.
It was Heartbreak Hotel on the gramophone.
It was Heathcliff by torchlight in bed after lights-out.

The dunes were molten glass. We slowed to a dawdle,
rippling sand with our toes, grains of gold
through our fingers, on our skin, in our hair,
without words to say why, or who, or where.

This I remember. The hour was still, bees
browsing sea-lavender, and beyond the dunes

the channel as blue as the Gulf of Araby,
a name from the drowse of a day-dreaming lesson,

sun on the board, the chalk, Sister's hand, a far-away
voice, as if heard through water, murmuring rosaries:
Egypt, the Red Sea, the Bitter Lakes, Suez.
A psalm of biblical names called Geography.

That was the last day the world stood still. In a year
there'd be tanks in Budapest, over Sinai bombers on
    the move,
and I'd be in the streets on the march against war,
as Empires loosened their grip. It was almost like love.

1956

DOUGLAS DUNN

Class Photograph

We were Elizabethan girls and boys,
Too young for politics, too old for toys.
Then Hungary and Suez changed all that,
Or so it feels in tired old retrospect.
Nostalgia corrodes the intellect.
It makes you want to eat your coat and hat.

One foot in childhood, one in adolescence,
Rock Around the Clock made far more sense
Even than *The Battle of the River Plate* –
Stiff upper lips and Royal Navy dash,
Its Technicolored brio and panache
Heroic, gore-less, brilliant, out of date.

Like Ovaltineys in their Start-rite shoes –
It catches up on you, it really does,
This looking back, this old class photograph.
Be-blazered in our uniforms and ties
(*Who he? Who she?*) – pensioners in disguise
As who they were, a pictured epitaph.

Pillar-boxes still red (though not much else is)
And the scarcely visible orthodoxies
All still in place, plus global urgency,
Destructive wars abroad . . . And yet, God bless
Democracy, dissent, and the NHS
Which underpins our civic decency.

1957

ELAINE FEINSTEIN

On not dying young

In blinding sunlight on streets wet with rain
    I brought my first son home
into our shabby flat near Free School Lane.

It was Cambridge weather: late February,
    a cold wind at the sill,
and shillings needed for the gas meter.

You were fixing the radio, preoccupied
    with plugs and trailing wires.
I let my body feed our sturdy child.

When was it, maybe ten days later ?
    that sudden flood of red –
a lake of blood on the bathroom floor,

then a stretcher under the stars, and voices:
    'The idiots left a swab inside her.'
'Will she live?' I counted down to four:

Death hath ten thousand several doors
         I would not enter,
waking, with my left arm strapped to a board.

They brought my baby to me when he cried,
         I was too weak to hold him,
but my milk still flowed. And you were there,

whispering, while I drowsed, breathing
         the newly unfamiliar scent
of that wild flower – *life*.

1958

MICHAEL LONGLEY

1958

I lodged above a poetry collection, all
The Irish poets accumulating on Victor
Leeson's shelves in Dublin's Wellington Road,
Reflections in his shiny baby grand.

Bach preludes, Pears toilet soap, bacon smells,
My melancholy first Michaelmas Term,
Cycling to rediscover Nausicaa
In Stanford's class, Odysseus hiding his sex.

Over breakfast Victor said nothing at all
And I had little to say. 'Two eggs please.'
No poetry yet, none of that craziness,
Calypso, Penelope, where were the girls?

Greek Verse Composition and Latin Prose,
Conundrums, three-dimensional crossword
Puzzles, I banged my head. 'The beautiful
Things are difficult,' Stanford quoted.

The Latin love-elegy came true for me
Eventually, when I held her hand
During *Les Enfants du Paradis*
In the Astor cinema along the quays.

Fifty years later, in the catalogue
Of Victor Leeson's poetry books, I find
Like a digamma my name, and we talk
In silence over the breakfast table.

1959

GEORGE SZIRTES

Meeting Walt

The year of Cuba and Sleeping Beauty, it was
my third year to heaven in a London Primary
with Mrs Haynes on dinner rounds, her summary
justice a smack with the spoon, reminding us
of virtue and the starving multitudes.
Dry pastry, streaks of grease, and scalding tea
in plastic cups – the cost of living in the free
world and cheap at the price. My father chewed
raw steak, my mother swam in garlic. Time
was lost in yellow smog, public monuments
still blackening in post-industrial grime.
We were the Empire and the map was ours.
We'd left behind our native tenements
For Walt, Fidel, at home with the Great Powers.

1960

ROY FISHER

The Air

Out of the air
and back again.
Nowhere to perch. Towers
and half-towers pushed up on the sandstone
balancing fantasy cafés on their corners
with fantasy rooftop vistas across the air.

Experience: by precept and long habit
to avoid if it sits in wait; to evade
if it comes on hard. To absorb
by osmosis without effort. Observed
of an afternoon standing oblique to the crowd
in mild catatonia under a bus-stop canopy
or in the vast hangar of the rag market
sure that among the greasy stalls
was the private oracle that would grab,
not to be evaded, and give a full sight of the engine
that was dropping out grown-up delinquents,
derelicts, junk. And sometimes

in the night places
or on the edge of a party gathered
round an epileptic in a pavement fit
one or two other faces, bewildered
but under compulsion. Writers.

No double depths, no oracle, no
Grand Encounter. Nature
and economics. Just eyes occasionally glinting
from quartz-veins in pebbles, stone scribbles
that didn't need reading. And the year's purpose
breaking apart in gobbets of prose. Accidentals.

1961

GEOFFREY HILL

Between the Cherubim

Tygers brush their compunction, sad drummer.
Our beat so to be beaten. Coventry's
unlaunched Odeon hangs in its gantries.
Remind me, now, who died that November.

Off-rhyme a law to itself. Nonsense. It
serves a turn. There must be comedians.
There does not have to be an audience.
I had not forgotten that death. Hence wit.

There is no true feeling without structure.
This may have been disputed. I recall
nothing from that tagged year I would wish ill.
Viewed through communal smoke a bad picture.

If we had birth it roared at discretion
of my wise child: a challenge to his time
so well served by the dealers of mis-fame.
This hiss of truth within thick air's secretion

I owe him for his love. And fabulous
Music probably there was; and justice
in fair measure; as ever malpractice,
trashy stuff cemented into fables.

1962

BRIAN PATTEN

Sixteen

Sixteen, Rimbaud and Whitman my heroes
'PS I Love You' playing in the loud cafés
In a Canning Street basement Adrian Henri
Painting *The Entry of Christ into Liverpool*

Adrift in an attic, in an ark buoyant with longings,
A map drawn by Garcia Lorca open before me
There was nothing that was not possible
Nothing that could not be reinvented

Ah poetry, at sixteen
Words smelled of tulips and marigolds
Their fumes made sentences
That the bees stole for themselves

1963

RUTH FAINLIGHT

World Events

Nineteen sixty three: Kennedy is
assassinated, The Beatles release their first
album, and Valentina Tereshkova
floats weightless against a faint radiation
from the final remnants of the Big Bang –
the first woman in space.

I had to Google 'world events' for that year,
but there was no problem remembering
what I'd been doing.

We travelled back from Morocco, because
Alan was invited to Russia, and now that Ted
had left her, Sylvia and I planned to spend
that month together in North Tawton
with our three babies (and my nanny
to make it possible), talking, walking,
and writing poetry.

I was the new mother: my son a few months
the younger; but she already had a daughter,
plus a published first collection – which made
me feel competitive, and I didn't like that! –
although she envied my glamorous life,
she confessed. But we acknowledged so much
in common, with delight.

That poetic meeting never happened, yet
I dream about it. What more to say? Everyone
knows the story's ending.

Credit cards, Valium, cassette tapes,
remote controls for TV: developments
of nineteen sixty three. And more events.
Now each protagonist of this sad tale,
bar me, is dead – yet all of us are blessed:
we live through poetry.

1964

ROGER MCGOUGH

Events & Happenings

It began like any other, trying to draw attention to itself.
Jumping up and down, 'Look at me, look at me.'
But once the smoke had cleared, bells fallen silent
and auld acquaintances forgot, what do I remember
of sixty-four? Race riots, the jailing of Mandela,
Vietnam, Harold Wilson, the last hanging in Britain,
the Beatles, and of course, finding you.

~

Evenings we'd spend together in the cellar bar below
Venture upstairs occasionally to watch a theatre show
Events and Happenings, poems on Monday nights
Read by wistful beatniks fed on City Lights
Young, we talked of freedom, pop art, CND,
Miniskirts and football, and we danced to R&B,
At midnight we'd wander home with dreams enough
   to spare
Now I wander still down Hope Street but you're no
   longer there.

Liverpool 8

While we sleep, heads in the clouds, who drops kicking
    into history?
A quarrel over money, murder, a medallion left at the
    scene.
Local girl Norma points the finger at Peter and Gwynne.
    Sorry lads.
Two trapdoors open for the last time with macabre syn-
    chronicity.
On the other side of the East Lancs, a mirror image.
    Strangeways.
No dreams to spare. Nightmare, a tumbril's ride from
    Hope Street.

                                   Liverpool 9

1965

GRACE NICHOLS

Sweet Fifteen

If the leaves of my memory serve me –
That was the year my hair went bee-hive
the year of the kiss, touching smugly
in the mirror my bee-stung lips.

If the branches of my memory stir me –
That was the year I fell in love with Otis,
his soulful syncopated R-E-S-P-E-C-T
each letter reverberating me to bliss.

For certain it was the year History rooted me –
Mr Owen, our history teacher – clad only in an armour
of trousers and rolled-up white sleeves – rescuing
   History
single-handedly from dates and dusty treaties.

Giving the kiss-of-life to the leaden text –
Resurrecting from the pages the long gone dead –
Interweaving the *Treaty of Tordesillas*
with jokes about he and his dear, Mrs Owen.

How once she took such an age getting dressed,
that when she finally descended, all set,
his chin had grown hair and he had to shave again.
Then it was back to battles; islands claimed; renamed.

Thank you, Mr Owen for the perks of your words
Thank you, Otis Redding for rocking my world
Thank you bee for my hive and my bee-stung lips
Thank you mirror for the buzz of that kiss.

1966

LIZ LOCHHEAD

Photograph, Art Student, Female, Working Class

Her hair is cut into that perfect slant
– An innovation circa '64 by Vidal Sassoon.
She's wearing C&A's best effort at Quant
Ending just below the knicker-line, daisy-strewn.
Keeping herself in tights could blow her grant
Entirely, so each precious pair is soon
Spattered with nail-varnish dots that stop each run.
She's a girl, eighteen – just wants to have fun.

She's not 'a chick'. Not yet. Besides, by then
She'll find the term 'offensive'. 'Dollybird', to quote
Her favourite mags, is what she aspires to when
Her head's still full of *Honey* and *Petticoat*.
It's almost the last year that, quite this blithely, men
Up ladders or on building sites wolf-whistle to note
The approval they're sure she will appreciate.
Why not? She did it for *their* benefit, looks great.

Nor does she object. Wouldn't think she has the right.
Though when that lech of a lecturer comments on her tits
To a male classmate, openly, she might
Feel – quick as a run in nylon – that it's
Not what ought to happen, is *not polite*,
She'll burn, but smile, have no word that fits
The insult, can't subject it to language's prism.
In sixty-six there's plenty sex, but not 'sexism'.

Soon: *The Female Eunuch* and enough
Will be enough. Thanks to newfound feminism and Greer,
Women'll have the words for all this stuff,
What already rankles, but confuses her, will seem clear
And she'll (consciously) be no one's 'bit of fluff'
Or 'skirt' or 'crumpet'. She'll know the rule is 'gay'
     not 'queer',
'Ms' not 'Miss' or 'Mrs' – she'll happily obey it
And, sure as the Pill in her pocket, that's how she'll say it.

This photo's saying nothing, is black and white, opaque.
A frozen moment, not a memory.
The boyfriend with the Pentax took it for the sake
Of taking it, a shot among many others, randomly,
To see how it would develop. Didn't imagine it'd make
An image so typical it'd capture time so perfectly.
How does she feel? Hey, girl, did it feel strange
To be waiting for the a-changing times to change?

1967

MIMI KHALVATI

Glose: The Summer of Love

But even in the summers we remember
The forest had its eyes, the sea its voices,
And there were roads no map would ever master,
Lost roads and moonless nights and ancient voices . . .
– DONALD JUSTICE, 'Sadness'

That was the year in Shawshank Prison that Red
was paroled and hitched a ride to Zihuatanejo,
little place on the Pacific. As Andy said,
'a warm place with no memory' to go to
after the battles, burials – JFK buried
at Arlington, the Six-Day War, Biafra
born only to die an infant death – with no
family, home, no baggage. So there they fled –
two men with a past in that long hot summer.
But even in the summers we remember

– and who'd forget the summer of love, the rallies,
Be-Ins, fighting for peace armed with guitars,
the Sioux, South Dakota in facepaint with hippies
wearing bedsheets, carnations, paper stars

and us in black leotards for our first sally
onstage swanning around in star-struck poses,
Ruth so fond, Rory foolish, Tusse, Barra,
like a sun, a moon, Julian who died and Jimmy? –
yes, even in those days of wine and roses,
the forest had its eyes, the sea its voices.

Little did I dream when we did our audition
I'd marry Paul one day and have his kids.
While Puppet on a String won Eurovision,
the Shah was crowned, Elvis himself got married,
I was dreaming, as Andy was of redemption,
of 'an entirely novel kind of star', a pulsar,
nebula, lightmap of some bright beloved.
Bright? Just as stars spun out of all proportion,
black holes were named, the Milky Way grew vaster
and there were roads no map would ever master.

Some of us fell from grace, others found fame,
fortune or sank quietly out of sight,
seen only by the forest. Back in Chalk Farm,
our rehearsal rooms, black-ceilinged, -floored, daylight
still flanked by blackout shutters and the same
backstairs, church portico, return bays, arches,
breathe through the dark thicket. I could take fright –
to end up here so lonely. That's why I came.
That's where I found you, friends, as age approaches,
lost roads and moonless nights and ancient voices.

1968

HUGO WILLIAMS

1968

Now that I've forgotten Brighton,
now that I can't remember
The King's Palace Hotel,
its pool hall and brothel,
Volk's Electric Railway
rattling over the shingle
on its way to Black Rock,
or the spray that flew in our faces
when we pulled the canvas up to our chins
for the ride on the speedboat,

Now that I've forgotten
Ali Baba's Forty Thieves
poking their heads out of urns
in the window of Louis Tussaud's,
Joe Hunter's Second Line
playing 'The Man I Love'
in the Pavilion Gardens, I feel sure
nothing remains of that weekend
but this old theatre-club programme,
so long it has to be folded.

1969

CHRISTOPHER REID

The Clearing

Was it Biba, or was it the schmatta bazaar
of Carnaby Street?
Did a narcoleptic sitar muddle the air
like incense,
or was there some more laddish beat?
The Stones? The Doors?
Had somebody pinned the Pirate Jesus face
of Che Guevara to the wall, or Waterhouse's
orgasmically grieving, teenaged Lady of Shalott?
No matter. What I do recall
is a clearing in the jungle, where, on a table,
half a dozen shallow pot-pourri bowls,
brimming with petal-coloured knickers,
encircled the bellied bulk
of an old, contemplative cash register.
Oblation? Prayer?
Or what?
Please don't ask me to explain, or to remember
anything else. I was there.

1970

KIT WRIGHT

The Year Nijinsky Won the Triple Crown

Oshawa-foaled in the boundless Dominion
    of Canada –
Great
Scott!

Was he the mightiest thoroughbred ever
    conceived –
Or
What?

Northern Dancer his sire
And Flaming Page his dam,
This matchless colt
Like a thunderbolt
Whizzed out of the bunch and WHAM!

Horse of the Twentieth Century!
All time King of the Flat!
No-one had seen

An equine machine
Accelerate like that!

The 2000 Guineas, the Derby and then
    the St Leger –
Ker-
ripes!
And up was the greatest jockey ever in silks
Or
Stripes:

The Long Fellow, Lester Piggott,
Beating the whole field down
Like a wave that's tidal –
On bit and bridle
Taking the Triple Crown!

Then peacefully put out to stud,
This superhorse was fecund,
Retired from that Annus Mirabilis
(By all sound judges reckoned):

The eighteenth year of Her Majesty
Queen Elizabeth the Second!

1971

DAVID HARSENT

MAD

It will be the rat, he told her, the rat that first emerges
    from the crud
and crap after the infinite rapture of the megaton strike,
    its head
slick with what it burrowed through, what fell, what kept
    it fed.

You and I will close and fuse, bone seared to bone, flesh
    folded in.
Our silhouette will print the wall, one subterfuge, one
    skin.
Joined as never before, but joined, as we would have
    wished, in sin.

~

There were men in the seas of the moon. The great hare
    lay dead.
What they seemed to speak were broken lines of some
    unbroken code.

What they seemed to hear was the voice of God howling
in the void.

Earth was a rolling abstract, its blue-white trappings
dense
in darkness. They named it *terra nullius*. They were
drenched
in starlight, dead light. They scuffed the dust as they
danced.

~

It's nine, he told her, can you see? Nine, which multi-
plied
by any number reduces again to nine – vows of the
woodland bride,
choirs of angels, fleshly portals, nine versions of the
road

to Gethsemane . . . Bad luck, of course, to dream in
nines
but it can only have been in sleep that I saw them,
rat-clones
in a whirlwind of ash, the city burn-out, the broken
stones.

1972

WENDY COPE

1972

1972 was the year
Of the hippy librarians from Islington.
My flatmate met hers first
And I got off with his friend.

They had beards. They smoked dope.
They were very alternative.
Mine gave me a copy
Of *Vedanta for the Western World.*

I wore long Indian dresses
And tried to like the smell of joss sticks.
In August we sat in bed
And watched the Olympics, stoned.

Late that year I went into analysis.
Freud didn't get along
With the hippy boyfriend.
We drifted apart.

It was fun, some of the time,
While it lasted. You could say that,
I suppose, about most years,
About most lives.

1973

JOHN AGARD

The Centenarian

Must get our dates right, mustn't we?
Now, did you say 1973?
How time fades into a blink.
No, don't tell me. Let me think. Ah yes,
wasn't that when President Watergate
began to drown himself in a pool of tape,
while Vietnam's eyes reddened the globe?
And somewhere, I remember, somebody
was killing somebody softly with a song.
Now a song would hardly scare a mugger.

In those days we clung to the hope
of the first of the last of the summer wine
and did our best to look on the bright side
of the dark side of the moon.
Pink Floyd, wasn't it? Saw him once on telly,
gutting a fish. My God, how times change.
Yes, it's all coming back to me. Back then,
we believed comets made breaking news,

and he who turned the water into vino
was turning into a billboard superstar.

The memory's not what it used to be.
But I can still tell nought from zero.
Zero . . . you know . . . wasn't he the one
who burnt while Rome fiddled?

1974

VICKI FEAVER

1974

It was the year Anne Sexton
sat in her red Cougar
with a glass of vodka,
behind the closed doors
of her garage, and drifted off
to its purring lullaby
in her mother's fur coat;

the year I read Emily Dickinson:
This is the Hour of Lead –
Remembered, if outlived,
As Freezing persons, recollect the Snow –
First – Chill – then Stupor – then the letting go –

'What do you do?'
a man asked me at party.
'What do you do in the afternoons?'

I was thirty-one:

the same age as Plath
when she turned on the gas.

I filled holes in the walls
and typed manuscripts
for a man who called me stupid
when I couldn't read his scrawl.

'I'm a poet!' I lied –
jolting myself to life:
a woman buried under ice
with words burning inside.

1975

ANDREW MOTION

The Convoy of Tears

When I came home unexpectedly in the mid-afternoon
and found an extra knife and fork still wet and glittering
on the draining-board beside your own, I knew at once.
I ran upstairs and called your name in our ruined
    bedroom

but you had already left. Soon afterwards I saw Margaret
Thatcher taking over the Tory party from Edward Heath,
and one evening – unless I was mistaken – the dead body
of P. G. Wodehouse borne on a tank into the ruins of
    Saigon.

1976

SARAH MAGUIRE

To a Ladybird

Out of mid air you alight on my blue linen shirt –
scarlet bead, blood drop,
uncut garnet.

We live in strange weather: clouds of you throng
our cloudless skies, sated
on aphids

fattened by a heatwave that plagues the withering roses.
And so we meet in a room
I will leave

in three months' time, its brickwork at bloodheat,
the tall sash window
flung open

on another airless, burnished night, as the exhausted city
sags into clay: cracks
in stucco,

graves parched ajar, the sump of the Thames coiling
through mudflats, lawns
now scrubland.

No one yet knows this is the longest drought since
    records began.
I do not know my broken heart
will be mended

to be broken again by the very same man a decade on.
I proffer you a fingertip and you scale
its length

to enter the rough landscape of my palm, heart line
    pierced
by fate, the undescribed arc
of the life line.

I cannot know I will write these lines half-a-lifetime later,
a few streets away. At this moment,
you pause:

let your shell bifurcate, unlatch your hatchback carapace,
unpleat the gauzy length
of your wings –

and whirr where you will.

1977

IMTIAZ DHARKER

1977 (I am quite sure of this)

Some Glaswegians still speak of the Silver Jubilee
and the Queen's cavalcade sailing off
from George Square on a sea of Union Jacks.
Others recall that around the same time
the Sex Pistols' *God Save the Queen*
was black-listed by the BBC

>   but what I remember is
>   that one night I danced in spangled
>   hotpants, with a boy in polyester
>   flares (I am quite sure of this),
>   in time, on track, one hand in the air,
>   one step forward, one step back.

Time is easily tangled. It falls over its own feet.
That year peeled itself as perfectly
as the rings around Uranus.
Smallpox was eradicated, miles of fibre optics
laid, personal computers offered to the masses.
People said it had never been so good

and what I remember is
the popcorn mix at Regal Cinema,
salt over sweet, the triumph of good
over evil, light-sabres slashing the air
in synchronised time, on track,
one step forward, one step back.

People said it had never been so bad,
Bengal hit by a cyclone, snow in Miami,
New York plunged into darkness.
and out of the sky a fireball fell on Innisfree.
People said it was a sign. And that was the year
Steve Biko died.

Other people died in other years, but that year
Groucho Marx and Charlie Chaplin died.
Jacques Prevert and Robert Lowell died.
In Memphis, Elvis died. Still,
someone called Roy Sullivan was struck
by lightning for the seventh time
and survived

but because of the odd way time unfolds,
what I remember is the last few seconds,
the countdown under a glitterball
(I am quite sure of this),
light flashing in your eyes

and your hair as you moved
in time, on track, one hand in the air,
one step forward, one step back,

and ah, ah, ah, ah,
staying alive. Staying alive.

1978

ALAN JENKINS

Between

Some time between *Plenty* and *Betrayal*,
Between Kate Nelligan in a black
Waisted plunge-line '50s dress
Looking me straight in the eye
When she took her bow, and the back
Of Penelope Wilton's mini-skirt,
As 'Jerry' clutched her arse,
Riding up dangerously high;

Between my last pair of denim
Hipster flares and my first
Pair of corduroy Oxford bags,
Between wanting to be taken for
The standard hippy-Fauntleroy
And the lost *Picture Post* boy
Who'd spat some lyrical venom
And died in the Spanish Civil War;

Between 'Night Fever' and 'Some Girls',
Between my monkish book-lined cell
And a bijou flat in Battersea
Paid for by the invisible man,
Between my last-ever Mandrax
And my first line of coke (I'd gone
Straight to drug heaven from drug hell),
Between invasion and peace plan;

Between a love I'd counted on
And the end of that self-flattery,
You were born, whom I met over *kir*s
Thirty years later. Between first kiss
And last, between offering your tail,
Your mobile number and email address
And administering the *coup de grace*,
You brought me to my knees. To this.

1979

MAURA DOOLEY

Life and Land, Thursday May 3rd 1979

> *Now Voyager sail thou forth to seek and find*
> – WALT WHITMAN

A spaceship spins a course from star to star,
netting Jupiter, to send home the fabulous,
a gossamer of gas dusting all the front pages,
as, far below, a Raleigh Olympus
slips down the morning lane, scythes
the long grass, turns on the face of a daisy
to trim the edge of the Selby coalfield
whose hedges brim and froth with blackthorn,
still frosty, meshed in web and filament.
A maiden voyage and who should be surprised
when the vote is cast, when the mark is made,
to feel in May that sudden snatch of snow
seen not as warning but as wonder,
not as presentiment but as a snatch of snow
by the young face lifted to ice and sunshine,
turning, as her wheels spin for home, steady
under the eternal shifting heavens.

1980

SUJATA BHATT

1980

It was the Year of the Monkey.
The Green Party was founded in West Germany.
Jean-Paul Sartre died, and the next day
my friend, Mary, said, 'I wonder how Sartre
feels now, because now he knows
that God exists after all.'
The people of India voted for Indira Gandhi.
The people of America voted for Ronald Reagan.
And then, John Lennon died.
It was the Year of the Monkey.

1981

JOHN BURNSIDE

Tommy McGhee, Corby Works

He had been there since '55,
his lungs thick with smoke
and urea, the wicks of his eyes
damp, like the walls
of the furnace he tended for years,
till they laid him off.
He'd thought he would be glad
to say goodbye;
but that last shift, walking away
with the cold flask and rolled-up newspaper
tucked in his coat,
he turned to the sudden black
where the ovens had been:
wet slag, and frost on the tracks
and the last sacks of by-product
shipped out to beet-farms
and landfill.
With severance pay
and two years to go
till his pension,

he'd money enough
to survive;
but he hated to see himself
idle, a man on his own,
his wife dead, his grandchildren grown
and moved away.
He rarely saw his son;
though, once, in a bar
on the Beanfield, he found him
sitting alone with *The Mirror*:
Natalie Wood had drowned
in the ocean, near Catalina,
a hint of champagne
on her breath, and the longtime
child star's bewildered smile
a memory now, as she stared up
out of the picture
and both of them, father and son,
remembered how, long ago,
they had almost
loved her, miming that song
about time
through her immigrant smile
that neither could disbelieve
as hard as he tried
– *somewhere, a time and a place* –
since there had to be something.

1982

SIMON ARMITAGE

Task Force

There the great gathered with gallant allies,
massing on the foreshore, fitted out marvellously.
Dukes and statesmen, some strutting on their steeds,
Earls of England, armies of archers,
stout sheriffs shouting sharp instructions
to the troops who rallied before the Round Table,
assigning soldiers to certain lords
on the seafront, in the south, at their sovereign's say so.
The barges being ready they rowed to the beach
to ferry aboard horses and fine battle-helmets,
loading the livestock in their livery and tack,
then the tents, the tough shields, tools to lay siege,
canopies, kit bags, exquisite coffers,
ponies, hackneys, horses-of-armour . . .
thus the stuff of stern knights was safely stored.
And when all stock was stowed they stalled no longer,
timing their untying with the turn of the tide;
ships of all sizes ran up their sails,
all unfurling at the moment of their monarch's command,

and hands at the gunwales hauled up the great anchors,
watermen wise to the ways of the waves.
The crew at the bow began coiling in the cables
of the carriers and cutters and Flemish crafts;
they drew sails to the top, they tended the tiller,
they stood along the starboard singing their shanties.

So the port's proudest ships found plentiful depth
and surged at full sail into changeable seas.
Without anyone being hurt they hauled in the skiffs:
shipmates looked sharp to shutter the portholes
and tested depth by lowering lead from the luff.
They looked to the lodestar as daylight lessened,
reckoned a good route when mist rose around them,
used their knowing with the needle-and-stone through
    the night,
when for dread of the dark they dropped their speed,
all the seadogs striking the sails at a stroke.

1983

FRED D'AGUIAR

The Year as a Muscle

1

Asked to pick up the slack of an island
Neighbouring a continent, that muscle
Flexes night and day through the year.

Weeks season into months, sweat and tire,
An ache grows in crooks at elbows, between
Shoulder blades and behind knee-plates.

Kind hands try but can do nothing,
For this year asks too much of muscles.

2

Seen from an ocean bed, the year subdivides,
Plankton hardens coral, so that on any two
Cardinal points, four tribes or three territories,
With a fourth as an offshoot, if history climbs
Aboard and sociology bails over the side.

A tunnel is not the answer so if you build it
Today somebody must fill, flood, or cave it in
Tomorrow with bare nails on wounded knees.

3
By this time the colony is a former lover
I spot early and cross High Street away from
The Greengrocer to skip her stony look or hiss

Under her breath, or worse, the smile of a sphinx
As her eyes burn through me turned plate glass.

That year, I made a string of naked promises
Like a decorated politician on the cusp,

Or put with spin, the year made me make them.

4
And that year set out to break them, each and every
Last one of them, dragging me down with it,

Me and some deer-eyed children learning Arabic,
Who press too hard on pencils time and again,
Blubber-blubber of said year at neck, wrist, groin.

I keep one hand in my pocket, fingers crossed
Just in case that former lover doubles back
On me and our eyes make four and we lock horns.

5

The year spreads five fingers, left hand,
Palm down, on Formica tabletop,
As right hand plunges an unfolded knife
Into the tremulous V between metatarsals.

This makes the year a sound, urgent
Raps on dressed wood by knuckle dusters,
Enough for neighbours to flick window nets, up
The TV, or plop the diamond stylus on a vinyl.

6

'Cathedrals to the dollar,' you said, as we marched
Away from the demo, through the city, in search of

A pint, past the Exchange, along Jamaica Alley,
Glancing up to avoid the raised tails of pigeons.

We talked against our age, its forest of cranes,
Camels with two humps on our back, race and class,

Or one large hump on two humpbacked whales,
And a chip (macro), cha! a bazooka, on our shoulders.

1984

ROBERT CRAWFORD

1984

I was in Oxford, donating my body
Every day to the Bodleian Library,
Claiming it back every night;
In love with a quick-witted laser physicist
Who told me stories of her Saigon childhood,
How one noon she'd watched a column of red ants
Filing to the stone where she crushed them.
Remote from the Miners' Strike, Greenham Common,
Mick McGahey and Margaret Thatcher's
Picket lines of the damned,
I plodded my way through the quad of the Bodleian,
Under the dour, Divine-Right eye
Of James the Sixth's sky-high statue;
But I wept hot tears, boarding a train
That took me away for the very last time
From the railroad station at Princeton, where
The physicist stayed; and I hardly noticed
Her lab's newest recruit, that freshly invented
Apple Mac whose cold, dry-eyed stare

Would render our clackety, typewritten youth
Old as King James. Nor did I foresee
You standing by me in time's republic
Today with our daughter, this dancing rebel
Rollerblading teenage reader
Yet to reach *Nineteen Eighty-four*.

1985

SEAN O'BRIEN

Another Country

Get there if you can
– W. H. AUDEN

Scattered comrades, now remember: someone stole the
  staffroom tin
Where we collected for the miners, for the strike they
  couldn't win,

Someone stole a tenner, tops, and then went smirkingly
  away.
Whoever did it, we have wished you thirsty evil to this
  day:

You stand for everything there was to loathe about the
  South –
The avarice, the snobbery, the ever-sneering mouth,

The lack of solidarity with any cause but *me*,
The certainty that what you were was what the world
  should be.

71

The North? Another country. No one you knew ever
    went.
(Betteshanger, Snowdown, Tilmanstone: where were
    they? In Kent.)

'People' tell us nowadays these views are terribly unfair,
But these forgiving 'people' aren't the 'people' who were
    there.

*These days your greying children smile and shrug: That's
    history.*
*So what's the point of these laments for how things used to
    be?*

Whenever someone sagely says it's time to draw a line,
We may infer that they've extracted all the silver from the
    mine.

Where all year long the battle raged, there's 'landscape'
    and a plaque,
But though you bury stuff forever, it keeps on coming
    back:

Here then lie the casualties of one more English Civil
    War,
That someone, sometime – you, perhaps – will have to
    answer for.

1986

ROBIN ROBERTSON

The Halving

Royal Brompton Hospital, 1986

General anaesthesia; a median sternotomy
achieved by sternal saw; the ribs
held aghast by retractor; the tubes
and cannulae drawing the blood
to the reservoir, and its bubbler;
the struggling aorta
cross-clamped, the heart
chilled and stopped and left to dry.
The incompetent bicuspid valve excised;
the new one – a carbon-coated disc, housed
expensively in a cage of tantalum –
is broken from its sterile pouch
then heavily implanted into the native heart:
bolstered, seated with sutures.
The aorta freed, the heart re-started.
The blood allowed back
after its time abroad, circulating in the machine.

The rib-spreader relaxed
and the plumbing removed, the breast-bone
lashed with sternal wires, the incision closed.

Four hours I'd been away: out of my body.
Made to die then jerked back to the world.
The distractions of delirium
came and went and then,
as the morphine drained, I was left with a split
chest that ground and grated on itself.
Over the pain, a blackness rose and swelled;
'pump-head' is what some call it
– debris from the bypass machine
migrating to the brain – but it felt
more interesting than that.
Halved and unhelmed,
I have been away, I said to the ceiling,
and now I am not myself.

1987

JO SHAPCOTT

The Great Storm

We rode it all night. We were not ourselves
then.

Through the window everything was horizontal.
In cars and ships and woods, folk died.
Small trees scattered like matchsticks
and a whole shed flew by. The world roared.
A branch broke into the kitchen,
strewed twigs into the banging cupboard,
filled broken crocks with leaves. I heard
a tricycle roll up and down the attic as
the firmament streamed through smashed tiles.

I loved you but I loved the wind more,
wanted to be as horizontal as the tree tops,
to cling to the planet by my last fingernail,
singing into the rush, into the dark.
I didn't know then I would watch
my beloveds peel off the earth

each side of me, flying among tiles, bins,
caravans, car doors and chimney pots,
watch them turn themselves into flotsam
and disappear as wholly as the pier
the next morning, a Friday, mid-
October. Gone, split, vamoosed
like the fifteen million trees.

1988

LACHLAN MACKINNON

1988

In the last full year of the second Reagan
administration, all seemed setting fair
for freedom. Noble dreams were coming true.

Zeks were trekking homeward from the camps
in their first fours and fives to find what faces
waited in villages now parts of cities.

From Petersburg to Vladivostok, troubled
small people were enjoying making trouble
for the brute, the berk and the bureaucrat.

They would soon learn about insurance scams,
the speed with which poems give way to porn,
the greed that keeps the market cycle turning,

but this was spring in Europe, cleaning house
with windows open to the songs of birds.
I'm grateful to have lived at such a time

and sorry truth exacts that I add this:
eighty-eight was also the last full year
of the red threat that kept our bankers honest.

1989

ROBERT MINHINNICK

At a Dictator's Grave

Someone has left dandelions
in a jamjar. One o'clock, two . . .

Yes, it's later than we think, now lover,
much later than we think.

Because this is what happens
when the old men make us wait.

And it crossed my mind in the cemetery
about the best way to behave:

how should I conduct myself
beside a dictator's grave?

Why not ragwort, lover? Ivy?
Or the corpse-colour of henbane?

But crowding round, the children laugh
as children always must,

I suppose they'll still be laughing, love,
when you and I are dust.

Yes it crossed my mind in the cemetery
about the best way to behave,

but why did I not use bare hands
to dig the dictator's grave?

I dreamed I saw our leader, lover,
as he was driven from the scene,

mottled like marble in the back
of a German limousine.

Yet all our lives we've had to drink
green water from the grave.

Yes it's later than we think, now lover,
much later than we think.

1990

PHILIP GROSS

Home

for John Gross

One day, in that year, and so quietly
that not the closest of us guessed,
      the history of Europe changed.

I don't mean votes and constitutions,
old flags in the attic half a century
      now tentative petals again,

but one day, one night out beyond
the houselights, beside one of those fires
      you would tend, and attend,

and chivvy patiently to sleep. (So many
leaves, that year, as if they were pouring in
      on quite another wind.)

It may be some recording angel, veiled
or given momentary body by a furl
        of smoke, might have seen

the moment when, thin blue letter in hand
saying *Come, you can come home now*,
        you knew: the place you'd dreamed

of going back to, with a family,
three horses, a path through the fields,
        was nowhere. *What could I do*

by going, you said later, *except see*
it was gone? Blue paper crinkling in the fire.
        Estonia was safe, here, inside you.

1991

ANTONY DUNN

Eighteen

York, 25–6 June 1991

These are the longest days. Exams are done
and we are indolent and steeped in sun
and somewhat drunk by dark, one couple gone
to fumble, inexpert, beyond the lawn
and the reach of the bonfire, when someone
cries 'Midnight'. It's the twenty-sixth of June.
I am sung to an end; I am begun.

Tifanny, Rachel, Joby, Simon,
Michael, Sally, Charlotte, John.

We lie back in the ordered grass as smoke
riddles the machinery of trees, tracks
east across the fields, and east. Someone cracks,
'It might be ours to go and not come back,
drafted to Sarajevo or Iraq.'
We can't make each other out. No one speaks
but someone pokes the fire and scatters sparks.

Adam, Isla, Sophie, Kinshuk,
Indraneil, Becky, Mark.

We have exhausted everything that burns
bright and quick and the fire has guttered down
to a smallness of embers before dawn.
A blackbird starts at a rumour of sun.
The day will come along the green dark lane
with processing cars to carry us on.
We will not be this way again.

Tifanny, Rachel, Joby, Simon,
Michael, Sally, Charlotte, John.

1992

MONIZA ALVI

Marlene Dietrich

(1901–92)

If she were just a voice, and if
there were no black sequinned gown
no trailing white fur
no signing of a soldier's cast,
just a voice, and a name
an eleven-year-old spliced together
from Marie and Magdalene,
Mar-lene, as two selves might fuse,
if she were just a voice
and not a sexual woman-man
with a top hat and tuxedo,
a voice that could break the heart
in different languages
create its own time of day,
a sliding, sultry, caressing
immaculate voice
that could make a throat of any room –

there'd be no performance in her 70s
no legs that were not as they were
no temporary face-lifts
no burial in Berlin-Schöneberg,
if she were just a voice
vibrating on the wind.

1993

IAN DUHIG

Fermat's Lost Theorem

*Mathematics is not a careful march down
a well-cleared highway, but a journey into
a strange wilderness, where the explorers
often get lost.*
– W. S. ANGLIN

Lisping numbers, poets don't count well;
we'll get lost in translational symmetry,
or looking for the bar in Hilbert's Hotel –
or in amazement, as on a day in 1993.

While we gawped at his magic solution,
Wiles stood back from what he'd done
like some alchemist out of Ben Jonson,
his name made, looking after number 1.

We know about vanity, but he got lost
in that labyrinth with one straight path.
'I think I'll stop here,' he'd said at last,
(proving wrong too, in the aftermath).

His maths would be rescued by friends;
still, we lettered monkeys of poetry,
with numerberless magical formulae,
type infinite A–Zs to infinite dead ends.

1994

PATIENCE AGBABI

Chunnel/Le Tunnel sous la Manche

Me, I was hard, rock hard: chalk marl, rock, la craie bleue,
la craie de la craie bleue: sea bed, *her* bed, la Manche.
Men fell in love with blue, fell fathoms deep in her
and saw my grey-blue face, my opening, my launch.
Moi, j'étais difficile, unyielding, hard to get.
The men, they craved me more, too dangerous, too dear;
from Shakespeare Cliff they craved deep down and, from
   Sangatte,
Europa's sisters carved down deep. They first kissed here:

here, in this place where first I felt that stab of air,
l'air frais, bore through me whole, and I became its form;
a structure sous la Manche, a sculpture sous la mer.
From cliff to breath, from la to le, I was reborn.
And now I am complete, put history on ice,
salute me in two tongues; come, kiss me, kiss me twice.

1995

GLYN MAXWELL

1995

You've an appointment with It
but you've not seen It in aeons,
so you text outside Its office.
Its assistant gets you coffees.

Then the door opens, there It is
indignant you were waiting
so It scolds the sweet assistant, saying
Bring him in for Christ's sake!

Then you're waiting on Its sofa
for It's still not done with business
but It grins at you from time to time
as if this was more interesting

than trading in sweet nothings
with Its tidying assistant.
Yet it's clear that any moment
It will let you in on something.

It is wondering and nodding,
as It holds as if in balance
two documents in two hands
This happened AND this happened?

And It wants you very much to ask It
What did, oh, what happened?
But you sit there, you do nothing,
It will tell you, It will tumble out

Kobe Sarin Sampoong
Sarajevo Srebrenica
Oklahoma Baku-Metro
Typhoon-Angela Serkadji

And the more It wants astonishment
the more you watch the window
as the names go by like floats do
some day you don't believe in,

don't celebrate or circle . . .
You gaze out at the great trees.
The rustling you hear
is It taking quiet offence now

as It files away the documents
and mutters for good measure
First detected: Sudden Oak Death.
Phytophthora Ramorum.

1996

MICHAEL SYMMONS ROBERTS

The Party Wall Act 1996

Something there is that doesn't love a wall
– ROBERT FROST

What divides us? Language,
habit, shyness, levee, breeze-block,
rockwool, horsehair, plaster, lath . . .

From now on, regard yourself joint
owner of a whole wall, not sole owner
of the half that bears your wallpaper.

Rest your ear against the cold
and eavesdrop on the dark interstice
separating your domain from theirs.

That sheet of stillness held between
the bricks is neither in nor out,
no fixed abode, a no-man's-land

of silverfish and woodlice, cross-hatch
of cables and the sharp ends of nails,
neither one world nor the next,

a space where all your cries and songs
crossfade with theirs – where
you and your co-owner harmonise.

From now, like Pyramus and Thisbe,
see cracks as conduits for words of love,
for breath, for perfume. Press your lips

against the rictus in the plaster,
cross the threshold with a whisper,
answer now: *who is my neighbour?*

1997

DON PATERSON

The Big Listener

Midnight. Connaught Square. A headlight beam
finds Cherie just back from her speaking date.
She looks at you. Less animal of late.
You lose no sleep but wake within a dream.
Your favourite: that old divided dark;
the white square at your neck; your good ear bent
towards the long sighs of your penitent.
You rinse a thousand souls before the lark
and wake refreshed, if somewhat at a loss
as to why they seem so lost for words.
They are your dead, who still rose to the birds
the day we filled the booths and made the cross,
before you'd forced them howling to their knees
to suffer your attentions. Spare us. Please.

1998

JEAN SPRACKLAND

International Year of the Oceans

Our grandparents lived
with a romantic moon.
They translated its faces,
raised imaginary ladders
towards its oceans –
Sea of Vapours, Sea of Nectar,
Sea of Serenity.

Our parents used the word *satellite*.
The seas were dry craters,
unreflective places, like dents
in a ball of crushed foil.
Impossible distances shrank,
and the moon was a scrap yard
littered with burnt-out metal.

Now Lunar Prospector
extends a fibreglass limb,
probes the polar cold-traps

and sniffs out atoms of ice –
frozen breath from the mouths of comets
lying where they crashed
in perpetual shadow.

Our children might harvest that ice
and live there as refugees.
Our grandchildren might set up camp
on one of Jupiter's moons,
where under a crust of ice
thick as a continental shelf
a warm ocean sleeps.

Will they train their telescopes
down the dark roads of space
on this lost blue world?
Will they tell the old stories?
How under the ice-cap our oceans teemed
with the great sleek bodies
of nuclear submarines.

1999

JACKIE KAY

Margaret Kirk née Baxter

When my grandmother died in 1999,
she was ninety one and a half,
old enough to add the half years
as she did when she was a wee lass.
1908, February, a leap year;
she was born in the middle of the night,
eldest of nine, from a long line.
My mum's mum – my mum was at her side –
she didn't make the millennium,
she died at the same time she was born
in the wee small hours, close to dawn.
She hailed from Fife, a miner's wife;
husband, twice buried alive
down Blairhall's Pit where he mined
the Ghost section, Diamond Stream.
The minute you went down that cage,
your life was in your hands:
a miner's life was no easy, and
neither was his wife's, your life flickered

up ahead like the miner's lamp.
In life, the light's not at the end
o' the lang tunnel; the light's inside.

When my grandmother's light sputtered out
before the century's close, the new millennium,
and the red curtain closed in the crematorium
she had the third eye, gifted before you die,
on the point of leaving the living for the dead,
she laid her weary head on the white pillow,
and said: *there will be nae mair tomorrows;*
I'm gled to be jumping ship. The future's
recession and depression; a'body's talking tae a screen.
The future's lonely. It's no for me.
I'm happy to be a has-been. She was hoary.
Outside the stars wrote her obituary,
a woman whose life *was less than ordinary.*
The nurse pulled the screen on her bed, said,
as if she were saying goodbye to an era,
They don't make them like that anymore.
The dawn light flooded in, my mum said,
as her beloved birds began a morning chorus
as if they were bidding her farewell, farewell . . .
My mum sat with her for a good while,
not far from the Campsie Glens, the Fintry Hills,
not far from the year nobody kenned whit to call.

2000

RACHAEL BOAST

Greenwich

No creature has been really comfortable
Beneath this turquoise dome
— HAFEZ

No year of years could ever
have come between
discomfort and pleasure
when they're hand in hand,
ancient as the hills of this borough
of the star and the hourglass.

High on the idea
of a new millennium,
we built only the shadow
of a dome, fated
to float midway on a wave
of its own unmaking.

In the mean time,
here's a reason to celebrate

which I'd call common sense;
the sense of the moon
going round the earth,
the earth

going round the sun
in a regal procession:
anyone under *this* dome
can find their here and now.
We govern by serving
that prime meridian.

2001

LAVINIA GREENLAW

Monolith

It was the fact of what happened.
It stood before us like a locked dimension.

We gathered numbers, rehearsed names,
stored a million images.

Still the door would not open.
There was no door.

It stood before us.
Featureless.

Neither beginning nor ending,
it was the new – blank, immoveable.

2002

IAN MCMILLAN

Saturday the Eleventh of August 2002

It's almost ten to three in the afternoon and the sun
Is just about holding its own in the Brillo Pad
Of the Bradford sky. It's the first game of the season

And you can taste the promise like lemon juice,
Like brown sauce on a crust. Ian McMillan
And his son Andrew can barely contain their joy

As they scuttle up the stairs to their seats. Then Ian
Overhears someone saying 'I've got
Three words for you: Ice Cream, Bike, and Cycle'

But that's four words, and in a moment the Barnsley
    players
Will rush out and get thrashed four-zip
And Ian McMillan and his son Andrew will leave

Before the end and go and sit on the supporters'
    coach,

Their heads in their hands. Own heads, own hands, of
    course.
But at this moment, before the match begins, those

Three (four) words hang in the air: *Ice cream, bike, cycle*
And they define the year. 2002: year of the words, wheels
Of the words spinning and melting slowly down your
    shirt.

Only two years into the decade
And already it's melting and spinning.
Pass me your head, Andrew: I'll hold it.

2003

COLETTE BRYCE

The Search

i.m. Jean McConville

1

Sand would swallow things,
would steal: a key,
loose coins, unnoticed
bits – a bottle
top, a silver
clasp – that no amount
of sifting would reveal,
no amount of delving
with a toy spade. The sand
withheld, kept shtum.

All day we searched
for Marion's wedding ring,
with a childish devotion
to the task. Marion,
in her post-natal sorrows,

back at the house, twirling
a lock of her hair
over and over
and over, that faraway
look. *Poor Marion.*

Close to the dunes,
we sifted, dug. One
patch of sand soon merged
with another. Not a land
mark, not a post, or rock,
the page of the beach
erased by the weather.
Our shadows loomed
on the lit strand,
conducting their own
investigation.

A small haul of items
amassed: a conch,
a twist of fisherman's
rope, the parched sole
of a shoe. Cloudy gems
of greenish glass; a picnic
cup, some patterned
cloth. At a loss,

we'd play, or bury
each other: feet, knees,
hips, chest; sand in our hair,
in our cuffs, in the turn-ups
of our jeans, sand
in the creases of our skin,
in our fingernails,
in the sieves of our fists . . .

2

In the nipped waist
of an hourglass, sand
begins to sift
a thirty-year wait

that ends with today's bulletin,
Jean: 'remains' uncovered
at Shelling Hill beach,
the deepest secrets
shallow after all. *Sand*
in the wind, in our eyes,
that will blind us

to tears . . . Your suffering
children are waiting,
older than you
by a good few years,

the names of your killers
hidden as yet
in the sand, that holds
together in the wind,

yet shifts
in infinitesimal layers
like truth, or ideology,
towards what history
must bear
in the altered light
of a new century.

2004

OWEN SHEERS

2004

1

Janet Leigh, actress, 1927–2004

I met her once, two years before she died.
LA in January on the Universal lots
and just the other side of those planes and towers
which had, already, made an after of everything.

Age had whittled her to a bird, the years
paring her at elbow, collar bone and cheek
so when she handed her coat to her driver
he draped it and half of her over his shoulder.

A cruel splice perhaps, for the photographer
to have taken her there. The motel unchanged
and the shower inside still the same
where, in fifty cuts and a single still,

113

her white-toothed scream, the sound of a knife
stabbing a melon, the shadow of 'mother',
all made, after the edit and the studio's campaign,
her name.

As she posed for the shots and I took my notes
a tour bus approached, the guide's voice amplified
through its windows – *And here on your right, the Bates
    motel,*
made famous in – Oh my god! It's Janet Leigh!

Their turning heads made her a starlet once more.
As the bus slowed down she switched on a smile
and released a red carpet wave, returned by twenty-four
palms pressed against glass, like convicts at visiting hour.

But as they drove on again, and she turned back to us,
whatever had lit her didn't last; the smile dropped
and her eyes downcast, as if she knew, already,
that more than just a bus had passed.

2
But none of us knew.
And even now we're still learning how much.
Look, here in the same magazine
where just last week I read of her death – this.

Another still; a young woman again,
her lips spread in a smile not a scream,
and her thumbs up as she leans into frame
to put her face beside the prone detainee's.

No lights, body doubles or make up.
No studio or Hitchcock composing the scene.
Just the flash of a camera in this place of ravens
illuminating this woman in fatigues,

this girl in a windowless corridor, unknowing,
like an actress in the seconds of a take,
that this moment, caught forever, will make her
    famous,
the new starlet face of American horror.

Photographs of the abuses and torture committed at Abu Ghraib
prison by the U.S. Army first came to light in 2004.

2005

JACOB POLLEY

The Box

THIS COULD BE YOU – IN A MUSEUM'
– BRITISH ARCHAEOLOGY, 82, May/June 2005

The curator leads you down
to the basement where the boiler squats
and lifts the lid from an unlabelled cardboard box.

So many are stacked in this
dry tunnel under the museum.
Upstairs: headstones, gold coins; down here:

bare brickwork, malevolent heat
and an unlabelled cardboard box.
The curator invites you to reach in

with both hands and ease
the miraculous bell
of bone from its unlabelled cardboard box.

There's a trickle of grit
in the hollow where the world was.
The loose teeth click

and suddenly you have your own
empty head in your hands, a code
in purple marker on the crown

telling where and when
you surfaced unexpectedly
as men were digging up the road.

2006

Love Poem Disguised as an Elegy

When I see you these days
you are always at a party,
standing by a window, alone,
growing younger and younger.
Heaven's great, you say.
You and Saddam are pals,
and from this distance,
everything is forgiven.
Do you remember when ...
But never mind.
It's always that last picture:
you propped up in bed,
your legs slightly raised,
the smell of piss,
purple sores,
a rebel body in disrepair.
Hush, you say, I have to go,
but remember, the heart
isn't a muscle, it isn't even a thing

that beats. It's what you love.
It's what you're doing today.

There'll be a time you grow
so young you won't know me,
and this is terrifying
because I still have things to ask
about the body and dying
and where memories go to live.
Just once, I'd like to see you
with the flower girls
back at the gate.
It wouldn't matter then,
if nothing like you
ever happened to me again.
It would have been enough
to have seen you change
into something small and golden,
charging off in to the waves
on your strong, white legs.
What need would there be
to speak of danger,
after you were gone, vanished,
like a dream into the day.

*for Chandralekha, who died on 30 December 2006, the same day that
Saddam Hussein was executed, also, the auspicious Hindu day of
Vaikuntha Ekadashi, when the gates of heaven are supposedly open to all.*

2007

HEATHER PHILLIPSON

Within the Cooling-off Period

Anti-essential days, a Thinker called them.
You might know we were in the new half
of the twenty-first century, enlarging
a pixel here or there without bursting anything.
SELENE Spacecraft had just blazed into the atmos.
3D goggles were en route to common usage.
My niece (not yet conceived), threw her huge
full-colour romper suit against the rough walls
of my imagination. It was like this: from a drop of water,
a logician could infer the Atlantic Ocean.

'Check it out!' – this was how people spoke –
'Your safety is in danger!' Visiting firemen
inspected our spoiled electric blankets with faces
with the look of faces about to be forgotten.
Safety, they implied, grows scarcer every second.
'Waskikkin, Firefighters? Multi-way plugs
in the overloaded bit wait for you
to bend and disconnect them.' Chockfull o' stories,

a fireman's arm in three dimensions
helped to make the present coherent.

Until then-then SELENE space-icles! Off
into lunar landscape to be a god, ciao-ciao!
A selection of feelings was contagious.
Via the National Grid, we shared experiences,
but we were alone at the sockets.
'Salvage me, Cookie!' – this aimed at the fireman –
'You, me, here in the riotous electrical pumping
of English winter. No. Hold it. Ich habe left a tap run-
     ning.'
I can't go into the meaning of all this, except to say
it was not clear if we were naked or pretending.

2008

CLARE SHAW

In the space of that year

14th January: I register her birth,
which is to say,
somebody writes it on paper. My face is a cave.
We walk round town but nowhere's open.

She hangs from me; small weight.
I'm meat,
heavier than you'd think was possible.
Each night, she drifts in her basket

through waves of colourless sleep
I can hardly believe anymore.
She's a small cat, curled at my chest,
searching for breast like air;

her mouth, its entire own creature.
Nobody told us a thing:
that mouth and its hunger
and nothing to fill it but me –

the mouth like a punishment – nobody warned us;
counting her life up
in gulps – fifty-nine, sixty –
in the open-and-shut (third time this night)

of her breakable throat.

~

World emerged
from the winter we willed her into,
its lights, its forests of noises
(she could not focus, she did not know us);

colour belled and pressed
like hands heeled hard against the eyes,
glowing like pain or clouds of stars;
like blood or Spring arriving.

World took shape in air and its textures;
she was pushed through or lifted;
she slavered and slept; she was still
and the silence was bees.

Her arms were Africa.
Her legs were Russia. Her back was
Here Be Monsters
and though there had always been voices,

it was out of the dream
world reached her;
with the cold plastic skin of a mat.
With light.

With hunger and faces;
the absence of water;
with dog, and the shock
of a sneeze.

She could not lift her own head.
She could not sit up
or eat. Could not speak.
She could not find her feet

until she did

2009

SINEAD MORRISSEY

Home Birth

13th February 2009

The night your sister was born in the living-room
you lay on your bed, upstairs, unwaking,
Cryptosporidium frothing and flourishing
through the ransacked terraces of your small intestine
so that, come morning, you, your bedding, me,
the midwife even, had to be stripped and washed.
Your father lifted you up like a torch
and carried you off to the hospital.

You came back later, pale and feverish,
and visited us in the bedroom in your father's arms.
You turned your head to take her in: this black-haired,
tiny, yellow person who'd happened while you'd slept.
And you were the white dot of the television, vanishing –
vanishing – just before the screen goes dark.

2010

LORRAINE MARINER

Eyjafjallajökull

I have always managed to get
to where I wanted to go to
eventually, have always assumed

that my destination would still
be standing when I arrived,
and I live in a city where babies

need passports; my Godson,
who only landed on this Earth
in April after airspace had reopened,

by October, was flying to Iceland
himself to be shown the Northern Lights.
So it seems perfectly reasonable

that a cricketer, whose team
was attempting to win some ashes,
should take advantage of a window

between Tests and fly 10,000 miles
and back in a week to be present
at the birth of his own jet age child.

*The ash cloud created by the eruption of the volcano Eyjafjallajökull
in Iceland in March 2010 caused the highest level of air travel
disruption since the second world war.*

2011

HELEN MORT

The Anthropocene

Move to designate new phase of geological time.
– GUARDIAN, June 2011

We've changed the world as much as asteroids
or earthquakes off-the-scale once did;
crafting an epoch on the sly, like a schoolboy
whittling a makeshift knife beneath a desk.

This era, shaped by what we never meant to last,
our accidental wars and numbered plastic bags. As if
the planet is a plane's black box, a record of what's
    thrown
or lost, the journey finished and the passengers all gone.

Today I stand on Helm Crag's summit, looking down,
the mountain's contours vague through fog that makes
each rock a secrecy. I squint until I think I see the earth
    below
imprinted with a map of all the scars, tattoos and
    birthmarks

in the world, graffitied with a list of who-loves-who.
Closer, the outlines of our outstretched hands
and closer still, part-sketch, part-score, a diagram;
the dream that stirs beneath each sleeper's face.

2012

CAROL ANN DUFFY

The Thames, London 2012

History as water, I lie back, remember it all.
You could say I drink to recall; run softly
till you end your song. I reflect. There was a whale
in me; a King's daughter livid in a boat.
A severed head
                    fell from its spike, splashed.
There was *Fire* –
birds flailed in me with burning wings –
Ice – a whole ox roasting where I froze, frost fair –
Fog – four months sunless, moonless, spooked by ships –
Flood – I flowed into Westminster Hall
where lawyers rowed in wherries, worried –
Blitz – the sky was war; I filmed it. Cut.
I held the *Marchioness*.
                            My salmon fed apprentices
until I choked on sewage; my foul breath
shut Parliament.
                    There was lament
at every stroke of every oar

which dragged the virgin's barge downstream.
Always bells; their timed sound, somewhen,
in my tamed tides, deep.

                         Caesar named me.

I taste the drowned.
A Queen sails now into the sun, flotilla
a thousand proud;
my dazzled surface gargling the crown.